WAY OF LIFE
LEADER GUIDE

WAY OF LIFE:
A STUDY BASED ON
THE GREAT SPIRITUAL MIGRATION

Way of Life Participant Guide

978-1-5018-4769-1
978-1-5018-4770-7 eBook

Way of Life: DVD

978-1-5018-4773-8

Way of Life: Leader Guide

978-1-5018-4771-4
978-1-5018-4772-1 eBook

The Great Spiritual Migration: How the World's Largest Religion Is Seeking a Better Way to Be Christian

978-1-60142-791-5 Hardcover
978-1-6014-2792-2 Paperback
978-1-60142-793-9 eBook

WAY OF LIFE

A STUDY BASED ON
THE GREAT SPIRITUAL MIGRATION

BRIAN D. McLAREN

**Leader Guide
by Lori Jones**

Abingdon Press / Nashville

WAY OF LIFE
A Study Based on *The Great Spiritual Migration*
Leader Guide

Copyright © 2017 Abingdon Press
All rights reserved.

This book is printed on elemental chlorine-free paper.
978-1-5018-4771-4

17 18 19 20 21 22 23 24 25 26 — 10 9 8 7 6 5 4 3 2 1
MANUFACTURED IN THE UNITED STATES OF AMERICA

Contents

To the Leader

To be human is to move. To be human is to change. Today, Christianity is in need of change. More specifically, Christianity is in need of a migration, says Brian McLaren. In *The Great Spiritual Migration*, McLaren lays out his strategy for how millions of Christian believers can save the faith. He explains three powerful shifts that define the change: a spiritual migration in which a system of beliefs is exchanged for a way of life of love, a theological migration that rejects a violent image of God in favor of seeing God as a renewing Spirit at work for the common good, and a missional migration concerned less with organized religion and more with organizing religion.

McLaren writes, "This isn't just a report of what's going on. It's an invitation for you to get involved, to come along, to help create a better future for our faith and for our world." In this study, we will explore what it means to join in this migration, and what it could mean for the longevity of our faith and how we can all become reflections of Christ in the world, working together for the common good.

HOW TO FACILITATE THIS STUDY

This six-session study makes use of the following components:

- The book *The Great Spiritual Migration: How the World's Largest Religion Is Seeking a Better Way to Be Christian* by Brian McLaren,

- The Participant Guide, *Way of Life: A Study Based on The Great Spiritual Migration,*
- *Way of Life* DVD, and
- this Leader Guide.

Participants in the study will need access to Bibles during the session; many activities will also require basic supplies including a markerboard (or large sheets of paper), markers, pens or pencils, and paper for each participant.

Each session is structured into a 60-minute format:

- Opening Activity and Prayer (5–10 minutes)
- DVD Segment (15 minutes)
- Study and Discussion (35–40 minutes)
- Closing Activity and Prayer (5 minutes)

HELPFUL HINTS

Preparing for Each Session

- Pray for wisdom and discernment from the Holy Spirit, for you and for each member of the group, as you prepare for the study.
- Before each session, familiarize yourself with the content. Read the study book chapter again, and read through the session in this Leader Guide.
- Choose the session elements you will use during the group session, including the specific discussion questions you plan to cover. Be prepared, however, to adjust the session as group members interact and as questions arise. Prepare carefully, but allow space for the Holy Spirit to move in and through the group members and through you as facilitator.

- Prepare the space where the group will meet so that the space will enhance the learning process. Ideally, group members should be seated around a table or in a circle so that they can see one another. Movable chairs are best so the group can easily form pairs, or small groups, for discussion if your group is large.

Shaping the Learning Environment

- Create a climate of openness, encouraging group members to participate as they feel comfortable.
- Remember that some people will jump right in with answers and comments, while others need time to process what is being discussed.
- If you notice that some group members seem never to be able to enter the conversation, ask them if they have thoughts to share. Give everyone a chance to talk, but keep the conversation moving. Moderate to prevent a few individuals from doing all the talking.
- If no one answers at first during discussions, do not be afraid of silence. Count silently to ten, then say something such as, "Would anyone like to go first?" If no one responds, venture an answer yourself and ask for comments.
- Model openness as you share with the group. Group members will follow your example. If you limit your sharing to a surface level, others will follow suit.
- Encourage multiple answers or responses before moving on.
- Ask, "Why?" or "Why do you believe that?" or "Can you say more about that?" to help continue a discussion and give it greater depth.

- Affirm others' responses with comments such as "Great" or "Thanks" or "Good insight"—especially if it's the first time someone has spoken during the group session.
- Monitor your own contributions. If you are doing most of the talking, back off so that you do not train the group to listen rather than speak up.
- Remember that *you do not have all the answers*. Your job is to keep the discussion going and encourage participation.

Managing the Session

- Honor the time schedule. If a session is running longer than expected, get consensus from the group before continuing beyond the agreed-upon ending time.
- Involve group members in various aspects of the group session, such as saying prayers or reading the Scripture.
- Note that the session guides sometimes call for breaking into smaller groups, or pairs, if your group is large. This gives everyone a chance to speak and participate fully. Mix up the groups; don't let the same people pair up for every activity.
- As always in discussions that may involve personal sharing, confidentiality is essential. Group members should never pass along stories that have been shared in the group. Remind the group members at each session: confidentiality is crucial to the success of this group.

Session 1

A Better Way to Be Christian

PLANNING THE SESSION

Session Goals

Through this session's discussion and activities, participants will be encouraged to

- consider the need for Christianity to migrate spiritually, theologically, and missionally;
- think about how God is calling them to migrate in their spiritual lives;
- discover what it means to fight for our faith, not just for a system of beliefs;
- realize how the Lord has equipped us in this fight; and
- receive the call to move forward to transform our faith into one that mirrors the life and teachings of Jesus.

Preparation

- Read and reflect on the Preface and Introduction in *The Great Spiritual Migration: How the World's Largest Religion Is Seeking a Better Way to Be Christian* by Brian McLaren.
- Read through this session outline in its entirety to familiarize yourself with the material being covered. Be aware that there is a lot of material that can be covered within this session, so try to balance your discussion and group activity times. Choose the session elements you

will use during the group session, including the specific discussion questions you plan to cover. Be prepared, however, to adjust the session as group members interact and as questions arise. Prepare carefully, but allow space for the Holy Spirit to move in and through the group members and through you as facilitator.

- Read and reflect on the following Scriptures:
  Genesis 12:1-9
  2 Corinthians 5:7
  2 Timothy 1:14
  1 Timothy 6:12
  Jude 1:3
  Matthew 23:25-28
  Ephesians 6:10-18
  Matthew 13:1-3, 45-46
- Have a markerboard or large sheet of paper available for recording group members' ideas.
- Have a Bible, paper for taking notes, and a pen or pencil available for every participant.

OPENING ACTIVITY AND PRAYER (5–10 MINUTES)

As participants arrive, welcome them to this study. Depending on how familiar participants are with each other, you might want to spend a few minutes introducing yourselves and sharing why you were interested in doing this study.

Read aloud or summarize:

As we begin this study, we are going to start by talking about change, and the way humans have changed and adapted throughout the history of humanity.

For discussion (ask one or more of the following questions, depending on time):

- If you have studied your family's genealogy, what have you discovered about how your family got from one place to another? Do you have any insight into why they decided to move where they did? What did it mean for them to uproot and then put down new roots?
- What has been the physical migration of your life? If you were to track your physical migration from place to place, how would you describe your movement? Why did you move, or why did you stay?
- How would you describe your religious migration?

Opening Prayer

Lord, we are here today because we want more of you in our lives and in our religion. As we meet together today, guide our conversation, open our hearts, and give us ears to hear what you have for us to hear today. Speak to us, Lord. Move in us, and draw us closer to your heart every day. Amen.

DVD Segment (15 minutes)

Study and Discussion (35–40 minutes)

The Great Migration

Read aloud or summarize:

Brian McLaren's book *The Great Spiritual Migration* begins, "The human story is a tale of people in motion."

From the very beginning, humans have always been on the move, searching for the best places for them to be nourished and safe, living in the tension of when to settle down and when to move on. As they moved from location to location, and with each season, the people had to ask, "Do we stay, or do we go?"

Given our nomadic roots, McLaren turns the discussion in the DVD segment from physical migration to what it might mean to migrate spiritually. When do we stay, and when do we go? McLaren says he finds it strange how religious people tend to settle down and stop moving, stop dreaming, stop questioning, stop exploring. We tend to trade the adventurous pathway of following Jesus for the heavy architecture of the religious industrial complex.

In the introduction, McLaren makes a bold claim: Christianity is in need of change. It needs a migration from a system of beliefs to a way of life based on love.

For discussion:

- Imagine that two men move onto neighboring lands. One builds a castle to live in, while the other pitches a tent and settles in. What do you imagine is each man's philosophy or outlook on his life? What do you think each man thinks of the other and his choices?
- McLaren asserts that, when it comes to matters of faith, religious people tend to settle down and stop questioning and exploring. Do you agree with this? Why or why not?
- What do you think is the status of the modern church— does it seem to be static or fluid? How would you describe it?
- Do you think a spiritual migration is needed in Christianity? Why or why not?

Read aloud Genesis 12:1-9:

> *The LORD said to Abram, "Leave your land, your family, and your father's household for the land that I will show you. I will make of you a great nation and*

*will bless you. I will make your name respected, and
you will be a blessing.*

> *I will bless those who bless you,
>   those who curse you I will curse;
>   all the families of the earth
>   will be blessed because of you."*

*Abram left just as the LORD told him, and Lot went
with him. Now Abram was 75 years old when he
left Haran. Abram took his wife Sarai, his nephew
Lot, all of their possessions, and those who became
members of their household in Haran; and they set
out for the land of Canaan. When they arrived in
Canaan, Abram traveled through the land as far as
the sacred place at Shechem, at the oak of Moreh. The
Canaanites lived in the land at that time. The LORD
appeared to Abram and said, "I give this land to your
descendants," so Abram built an altar there to the
LORD who appeared to him. From there he traveled
toward the mountains east of Bethel, and pitched
his tent with Bethel on the west and Ai on the east.
There he built an altar to the LORD and worshipped
in the LORD's name. Then Abram set out toward the
arid southern plain, making and breaking camp as he
went.*

Genesis 12:1-9

For discussion:

- In Genesis 12:1-9, God says to Abraham, go to the place
  "I will show you." Abraham packed up his family and
  their home and set off, not knowing where he was going
  or what he would even do when he got there. He was told

to simply go, in faith that God had a path for him. And he went. What does it typically take for you to make a move? If you were Abraham, how do you think you would have responded? What would have to motivate you to go?

- When the Lord tells you to move, but doesn't reveal how things will turn out when you get there, how do you typically react?
- Second Corinthians 5:7 says, "For we walk by faith, not by sight" (NKJV). What do you think God is telling us in this verse about how we should live our lives?

Fighting for the Faith

Read aloud or summarize:

In the New Testament, Paul and Jude encourage members of the young Christian church to fight for their faith.

Read aloud 2 Timothy 1:14, 1 Timothy 6:12, and Jude 1:3:

> *Guard the good deposit that was entrusted to you—*
> *guard it with the help of the Holy Spirit who lives in us.*
> *2 Timothy 1:14 (NIV)*

> *Compete in the good fight of faith. Grab hold of*
> *eternal life—you were called to it, and you made*
> *a good confession of it in the presence of many*
> *witnesses.*
> *1 Timothy 6:12*

> *Dear friends, I wanted very much to write to you*
> *concerning the salvation we share. Instead, I must*
> *write to urge you to fight for the faith delivered once*
> *and for all to God's holy people.*
> *Jude 1:3*

For discussion:

- In these passages, what verbs stand out to you? Do these verses describe passive or strong actions?

Read aloud or summarize:

The verbs "guard," "fight," and "compete," used in these passages demonstrate the kind of strength and determination it takes to fight for one's faith. Both Paul and Jude use the same Greek word for "compete" and "fight": *agonizomai*. If you look closely, you'll see here the root of the English word *agony*. It's no mistake that Jude uses this word because it's the same Greek word often used to talk about the intense effort displayed in athletic events. This is no passive fight.

McLaren lays out a modern-day concern much like Paul and Jude's—Christianity has suffered at the hands of Christians and has become a rigid system of beliefs. The religion no longer reflects the simple way of life of love taught by Jesus. Note that Jude and Paul urge believers to fight for *faith*, not a *system of beliefs*. It's a race worth winning, and we as Christians should put our most intense effort forward, agonizing as it may be. Fighting for the faith means fighting with strength and determination.

For discussion:

- McLaren points out that Jude did not say to fight for a belief system but to fight for the faith. Why is this an important distinction to make?
- In what ways does fighting for the faith sometimes look like fighting *against* a belief system?

Read aloud or summarize:

In the Introduction of *The Great Spiritual Migration*, McLaren gives the illustration of the Coke and the can, in which he points out that because of marketing and personal experience, we know what to expect when we pop open a can of Coke and take a sip. But, he wonders, what if we popped open the can and it tasted nothing like we expected, if it tasted horrible instead? How then might we think about Coke? Would we dare to open another can? He writes, "A brand like Coke only has meaning because it is linked to an essential quality or qualities for a soft drink: taste—not the can. . . . And what are the qualities of Christian faith that really matter, regardless of the packaging?"

Read aloud Matthew 23:25–28:

> *[Jesus said,] "How terrible it will be for you legal experts and Pharisees! Hypocrites! You clean the outside of the cup and plate, but inside they are full of violence and pleasure seeking. Blind Pharisee! First clean the inside of the cup so that the outside of the cup will be clean too.*
>
> *"How terrible it will be for you legal experts and Pharisees! Hypocrites! You are like whitewashed tombs. They look beautiful on the outside. But inside they are full of dead bones and all kinds of filth. In the same way you look righteous to people. But inside you are full of pretense and rebellion."*
>
> Matthew 23:25-28

For discussion:

- What do you think most people today associate with the Christian "brand"?
- How do you feel when you read Jesus' words in Matthew 23:25-28? Do they convict you in some way?
- How do you interpret Jesus' words for us modern-day Christians? What are some things that are dirtying our

cups? What are some ways that we tend to clean up the outside but neglect what's less noticeable?

What You Love, You Protect

Read aloud or summarize:

In McLaren's first devotional in the *Way of Life Participant Guide*, he talks about living near the ocean, and of how he and other residents work each year to protect sea turtle eggs, which are laid on nearby beaches. In order to survive, these eggs need protection from external threats such as raccoons, hurricanes, shrimp nets, water pollution, and other forms of human interference. These animals face external, not internal, threats. In the same way, he points out that, though in many places around the world Christianity *does* face real external threats, for the most part, the survival of Christianity is being threatened from within the faith. He writes,

> We Christians, you might say, are the greatest threat to Christian faith. Christians can be blinded by wealth and greed, misguided by religious or political leaders, polluted by un-Christ-like attitudes, kidnapped by ideology, or numbed by comfort and apathy. As a result, we can receive and pass on versions of the faith that are distorted with racism or twisted by greed or fear.

McLaren says that if we love our faith, we must protect it from dangers like these. And if previous generations have led us astray, we must have the courage to correct the course.

For discussion:

- McLaren points out that Christian faith is what Christians make of it—ugly or beautiful, judgmental or gracious, complacent or energetic, selfish or generous. What, do you perceive, is the current state of Christianity in our country?

- Do you think we are in need of a course correction? In what ways?
- What does it mean for you to fight? What's been your experience when you are frustrated or angry? Do you want to give up and retreat? Do you get angry and mobilize? What are your current feelings about fighting for the state of your faith?

We Are Equipped

Activity:

Read aloud Ephesians 6:10-18:

> *Finally, be strong in the Lord and in his mighty power. Put on the full armor of God, so that you can take your stand against the devil's schemes. For our struggle is not against flesh and blood, but against the rulers, against the authorities, against the powers of this dark world and against the spiritual forces of evil in the heavenly realms. Therefore put on the full armor of God, so that when the day of evil comes, you may be able to stand your ground, and after you have done everything, to stand. Stand firm then, with the belt of truth buckled around your waist, with the breastplate of righteousness in place, and with your feet fitted with the readiness that comes from the gospel of peace. In addition to all this, take up the shield of faith, with which you can extinguish all the flaming arrows of the evil one. Take the helmet of salvation and the sword of the Spirit, which is the word of God.*

> *And pray in the Spirit on all occasions with all kinds*
> *of prayers and requests. With this in mind, be alert*
> *and always keep on praying for all the Lord's people.*
> *Ephesians 6:10-18 (NIV)*

Using a markerboard or large sheet of paper, first make a list of the pieces of armor described in this passage. Then go back and, next to each piece of armor, have participants identify what Scripture says each item represents. (If you need help, see the list below.)

- Belt—Truth
- Breastplate—Righteousness
- Footwear—Readiness; Peace
- Shield—Faith
- Helmet and Sword—Word of God

Ask:

- What does the list above tell us about how God has equipped us? What tools has God given us to fight with?
- Considering the current fight for your faith (or Christianity as a whole), which part of the armor feels most vital to you right now?

The Call Forward

Read aloud or summarize:

In the DVD segment, McLaren says that *The Great Spiritual Migration* is a challenge to Christians to wake up, climb out of our ruts, venture out of our temples and tombs, and hear the call to migration arising in our souls. The call of this book, and this study, will lead us through three migrations needed to transform Christianity:

1. spiritual—moving away from a system of beliefs and toward Christianity as a way of life of love,
2. theological—thinking anew about Scripture and rediscovering a vision of a loving God, and
3. missional, or practical—going from an organized religion to a religion organizing itself for the common good.

(*Note to Leader:* You might want to write these three migrations on a markerboard or large sheet of paper for the group to see.)

Read aloud Matthew 13:1-3, 45-46, and (once again) Jude 1:3:

> *That day Jesus went out of the house and sat down beside the lake. Such large crowds gathered around him that he climbed into a boat and sat down. The whole crowd was standing on the shore. He said many things to them in parables: . . .*
>
> *"Again, the kingdom of heaven is like a merchant in search of fine pearls. When he found one very precious pearl, he went and sold all that he owned and bought it."*
>
> Matthew 13:1-3, 45-46
>
> *Dear friends, I wanted very much to write to you concerning the salvation we share. Instead, I must write to urge you to fight for the faith delivered once and for all to God's holy people.*
>
> Jude 1:3

For discussion:

- Some people interpret Jude's mention of a "faith delivered once and for all" as proof that Christianity is meant to stay the same throughout history. But in response to Jude

1:3, McLaren writes, "The message of and about Jesus is in fact a given—it is Christianity's pearl, our treasure, our gift, and it must never be lost. The meaning-rich stories of what Jesus said and did form the unique heart of Christian faith that must always pulse within us."

- What "meaning-rich stories" of what Jesus said and did are most important to your own faith? How would you summarize "the message of and about Jesus" in just one or two sentences?

CLOSING ACTIVITY AND PRAYER (5 MINUTES)

Leader, as you close each week's session, plan to take a few minutes for participants to quietly reflect on what you have discussed during this session. A reflection question or questions will be provided each week, along with a closing Call to Action, which participants will be invited to receive and engage in between meetings.

Read aloud or summarize:

McLaren points out that this call to forward movement is especially important at this moment in history, as many people are afraid and want to retreat into old ways of thinking. He says that *The Great Spiritual Migration* is a call forward into a just and generous form of Christian faith and discipleship that challenges us to become better people who live the good news of Jesus Christ in our daily lives.

- Where are you feeling God leading you to "migrate" in your faith and life experiences?

(*Note to Leader:* Take a few minutes for participants to quietly reflect on this question and journal their thoughts.)

Call to Action

Have some conversations this week—both with Christian friends and others who aren't a part of your faith community—about this idea that Christianity is in need of a spiritual migration. Perhaps ask a Christian friend to read the book along with you so you can discuss what you're reading. Ask a friend outside your faith community to give you their thoughts about Christianity being in need of change.

Closing Prayer

Living God, help us to discern your will for our lives and for our faith. Teach us to dismiss what is evil and cling to what is good. Give us the courage to leave behind anything that is holding us back from carrying out your will for this world and its people, whom you love so dearly. Help us together to embody and pass on a vibrant version of the faith that will empower future generations to live wisely and well. In Jesus' name. Amen.

Session 2

From a System of Beliefs to a Way of Life

PLANNING THE SESSION

Session Goals

Through this session's discussion and activities, participants will be encouraged to

- examine John's account of Jesus' revolutionary call in the Temple;
- consider what it means to live out of a system of beliefs versus living a way of life led by Christ;
- see the change needed in their own hearts and in their communities in order to follow Jesus' commands; and
- discover the way of life through the path of love set forth by Jesus in Scripture.

Preparation

- Read and reflect on "Part I: The Spiritual Migration: From a System of Beliefs to a Way of Life," in *The Great Spiritual Migration: How the World's Largest Religion Is Seeking a Better Way to Be Christian* by Brian McLaren.
- Read through this session outline in its entirety to familiarize yourself with the material being covered. Be aware that there is a lot of material that can be covered

within this session, so try to balance your discussion and group activity times. Choose the session elements you will use during the group session, including the specific discussion questions you plan to cover. Be prepared, however, to adjust the session as group members interact and as questions arise. Prepare carefully, but allow space for the Holy Spirit to move in and through the group members and through you as facilitator.

- Read and reflect on the following Scriptures:
    John 2:13-22
    Matthew 9:13
    Hosea 6:6
    Isaiah 43:18-19
    Matthew 22:36-39
    1 John 4:7-8, 12
    Hebrews 13:7
- Have a markerboard or large sheet of paper available for recording group members' ideas.
- Have a Bible, paper for taking notes, and a pen or pencil available for every participant.

OPENING ACTIVITY AND PRAYER (5–10 MINUTES)

For discussion:

- Last week's call to action was to have some conversations this week—both with Christian friends and others who aren't a part of your faith community—about this idea that Christianity is in need of a spiritual migration. Was anyone able to have one of these conversations, and if so, could you briefly share what that experience was like?

Opening Prayer

Living God, open our hearts and minds today as we gather together. Guide our conversation and help us to have the courage to ask the questions you've laid on our hearts as we seek to know more of you. In Jesus' name. Amen.

DVD Segment (15 minutes)

Study and Discussion (35–40 minutes)

The Jesus Revolution

Read aloud or summarize:

As McLaren points out in the DVD segment, the year 2017 marks the 500th anniversary of the Protestant Reformation, a radical call to reform the church made by a young priest named Martin Luther. Enraged by the political and social corruption of the Catholic Church at that time, Luther famously made ninety-five statements about how the church was misusing or abusing its position of faith and emphatically proposed a new way for people of faith to go forward.

Though today many Christians embrace Luther's beliefs, at the time, naturally, this action did not go over well with the established church. Nevertheless, many people believed and followed Luther's proposals, and the Protestant tradition began.

In the Book of John, we read of an important protest that Jesus himself made in the temple.

Read aloud John 2:13–22:

> *It was nearly time for the Jewish Passover, and Jesus went up to Jerusalem. He found in the temple those who were selling cattle, sheep, and doves, as well as*

those involved in exchanging currency sitting there.
He made a whip from ropes and chased them all out
of the temple, including the cattle and the sheep. He
scattered the coins and overturned the tables of those
who exchanged currency. He said to the dove sellers,
"Get these things out of here! Don't make my
Father's house a place of business." His disciples
remembered that it is written, Passion for your house
consumes me.

Then the Jewish leaders asked him, "By what
authority are you doing these things? What
miraculous sign will you show us?"

Jesus answered, "Destroy this temple and in three
days I'll raise it up."

The Jewish leaders replied, "It took forty-six years to
build this temple, and you will raise it up in three
days?" But the temple Jesus was talking about was his
body. After he was raised from the dead, his disciples
remembered what he had said, and they believed the
scripture and the word that Jesus had spoken.

John 2:13-22

Activity—Tell the Story:

Sometimes when we read a familiar Bible story such as this one, there is a tendency to zone out and not really hear the story. So in order to help the group be more engaged, help them hear the story anew and perhaps from a different perspective. If your group is small, ask two or even three people to retell this story in their own words. If the group is large, you might want to break into smaller groups and have one or two share in each group. Encourage group members to listen carefully and note what stands out to them during the retelling of the story.

After the storytellers have shared, ask, What stood out to you about each person's telling of the story? Did you hear or notice something new about the story?

Spend a few minutes thinking and talking about the scene—the sights, the smells, the crowds, and the noise. How do you picture Jesus as he enters the scene? As he is destroying the vendors' booths? What might the area have looked like after it was all over? How might those who looked on have reacted?

Read aloud or summarize:

During Passover, Jewish people from far away would journey all the way to Jerusalem to come to the Temple and offer sacrifices to cleanse them of their sins. Their journeys would have been long and strenuous, and most would not have been able to bring animals along with them for the sacrifice. Traditional interpretations about this passage, which is often called "the cleansing of the Temple," have claimed that the vendors were selling animals at exorbitant rates to worshipers who had no choice but to pay the costly price. Jesus, angered at the scene and that vendors were cheating the worshipers, chased away every animal there for sale. But, as McLaren points out, if Jesus were only worried about the poor having to pay for overpriced animals, why did he not leave the reasonably priced doves, which were also for sale? And why did he get so angry about this practice of selling animals for sacrifice, which was common and legal? His actions must have had a deeper meaning.

McLaren writes, "Jesus is making a revolutionary proposal: the Temple could crumble. It could pass away, and its collapse wouldn't be the end of the world." Instead, Jesus said, something new and better was coming, something better than their current system of beliefs about sacrifice and appeasement of God—"A system of extravagant and generous grace, open to all people," McLaren continues. "A more human, loving, embodied way of relating to God, self, one another, and all creation."

For discussion:

- How do you interpret this passage in John? Do you agree with McLaren's interpretation of the text? Why or why not?
- Read Matthew 9:13 and Hosea 6:6. How do these verses help to clarify Jesus' mission in this passage?

    Go and learn what this means: I want mercy and not sacrifice. *I didn't come to call righteous people, but sinners."*

    Matthew 9:13

    *I desire faithful love and not sacrifice,
        the knowledge of God instead of entirely burned
        offerings.*

    Hosea 6:6

- Do you think the Temple described in this passage could be a picture of the modern-day church? If so, how? Do you think the modern-day church's system of beliefs is failing?
- If you were a devout pilgrim present in this Temple scene, how do you think you would have felt to have Jesus passionately and violently destroy your long-held system of beliefs? How open are you today to the idea that your long-held system of beliefs might be in need of change?

Cracks in the System

Read aloud or summarize:

For many years, McLaren served as a pastor, and he struggled to reconcile the many growing questions and doubts he faced within the system of beliefs that defined his faith. One day he had a moment when he realized that, in order not to be a hypocrite and say and do what he did not believe, that he would have to let go of his system of beliefs altogether and instead seek to rediscover his faith anew.

For discussion:

- Have you ever had a moment when you could no longer hold your system of beliefs together (perhaps in regard to a job, a relationship, or a way of living) and everything needed to be reconsidered and remade? What came out of that experience for you?
- McLaren writes, "John's Temple protest story tells the truth: even if the worst imaginable thing happens, even if our traditional religious architecture crumbles—physically or conceptually—*even then* God can raise something beautiful from the rubble. The end is not the end. It's actually the doorway to a new beginning." What are some ways that fear can hold us back from the risk of moving forward?

Read aloud or summarize:

From the beginning, human beings have had a desire to be a part of something bigger than themselves—to belong. We have wanted to know who is against us and with whom we belong. We join with others that hold our same system of beliefs, and we reject those who will not claim those same beliefs. And so some are in (friends); others are out (foes). You might say this is the human survival strategy.

But what happens when we apply this same strategy to the Christian faith? McLaren writes, "Believing, it turns out, is more about belonging and behaving—and more about politics and sociology—than we typically realize."

For discussion:

- What is your reaction to this idea that our current Christian beliefs are often shaped by external social and political factors that have nothing to do with Scripture?
- How does your community of faith let people in, or keep them on the outside? What changes do you think are needed in your community in this regard? To what, or to whom, is your community loyal?

Read aloud or summarize:

Because change is hard for religious communities, McLaren encourages us to learn from science and the scientific method.

Beginning with a question, or something that needs clarification, scientists develop a hypothesis: a possible explanation they will then set out to prove. After countless observations and data collecting over time, scientists will then declare their conclusions facts. Those facts are then widely accepted and stand the test of time—that is, until *new* data comes along and challenges the fact. Scientists do not easily give up their facts but understand that new information demands they stay true to the scientific method and begin the process anew of answering the initial question.

We trust the scientific method because the method dictates that scientists must be willing to change their minds when necessary and be willing to tell how and why they came to those decisions. That method of transparency equates to believability. And, in order to be believable to the world around us, McLaren believes our religious communities should take our cue from science and be willing to change when necessary.

For discussion:

- Of his own journey, McLaren writes that the turning point for him was realizing that, in order to better follow Christ, he had to be willing to rethink what he'd always believed. What do you tend to think about people who are willing to change their minds? Why do you feel that way? How do those thoughts or feelings affect other areas of your life?

- Have you ever considered the idea that religion can change? How do you feel about McLaren's statements that it *should* be willing to change?
- Read Isaiah 43:18-19. What does this verse stir in you?

> *Do not remember the former things,*
>   *or consider the things of old.*
> *I am about to do a new thing;*
>   *now it springs forth, do you not perceive it?*
> *Isaiah 43:18-19 (NRSV)*

System of Beliefs Versus Way of Life

Read aloud or summarize:

McLaren writes, "For billions of people, for Christianity to be Christian, only one thing matters: *correct beliefs.* ... But as important as beliefs are, they are not the essential, unchanging, defining feature of Christianity."

Read aloud Matthew 22:36-39 and 1 John 4:7-8, 12:

> *"Teacher, what is the greatest commandment in the Law?"*

> *He [Jesus] replied,* "You must love the Lord your God with all your heart, with all your being, *and with all your mind. This is the first and greatest commandment. And the second is like it:* You must love your neighbor as you love yourself."
> *Matthew 22:36-39*

*Dear friends, let's love each other, because love is from
God, and everyone who loves is born from God and
knows God. The person who doesn't love does not
know God, because God is love. . . .*

*No one has ever seen God. If we love each other, God
remains in us and his love is made perfect in us.*
                                                    1 John 4:7-8, 12

For discussion:

- Based on these passages, what is the essential, unchanging,
  defining feature of Christianity?
- Have you ever known someone who professed to a system
  of Christian beliefs but who was not loving? How did
  you or others reconcile that person's system of beliefs and
  actions?

Activity:

What synonyms can you can think of for the word *love*? Have
participants call out these synonyms and record their answers on
a markerboard or large sheet of paper. (Some ideas are mercy,
peace, compassion, friendship, shelter, kindness, community, care,
and so on.)

For discussion:

- Which of these synonyms are descriptive of your faith
  community? How do they apply? Does your faith
  community have some work to do in this regard?

(*Note to Leader*: If time or interest allows, you might want to
brainstorm some specific ways that your faith community or group
can grow in love and in these characteristics listed.)

Read aloud or summarize:

Let's not miss the significance of Jesus' teaching in Matthew 22:36-39. Because he was addressing a faithful, religious people who held compliance with God's law above everything else, Jesus' message of love and his placement of love at the top of the list as most important was nothing short of revolutionary.

It's pretty ironic then, as McLaren points out, that Christians have used the name of Jesus throughout the years to separate, punish, and persecute those who don't conform to their same beliefs. The way of Christ should be our way of life, and that way is the path of love. Once we put love back in the center, everything will change.

For discussion:

- What do you think a "way of life/way of love" church would look like? What would it ask of its members?
- Paul writes, "Remember your leaders, those who spoke the word of God to you; consider the outcome of their way of life, and imitate their faith" (Hebrews 13:7, NRSV). Who are some people in your life who have modeled love for you? How have you sought to imitate their way of life? How can you reflect God's love to others in the same way?
- How might your life change if you put love in the center? How might your family or faith community change if you put love in the center?

CLOSING ACTIVITY AND PRAYER (5 MINUTES)

Leader, as you close each week's session, plan to take a few minutes for participants to quietly reflect on what you have discussed during this session. A reflection question or questions will be provided each week, along with a closing Call to Action, which participants will be invited to receive and engage in between meetings.

Read aloud or summarize:

McLaren writes that, "Faith and beliefs seem like the same thing to many people, but they actually differ in profound ways."

- In what areas of your life have you been living out of a system of beliefs? In doing so, have you been following Jesus? Where has *love* ranked in your loyalties?

Take a few minutes to quietly reflect on this question and journal your thoughts.

Call to Action

Read 1 Corinthians 13 (often dubbed "The Love Chapter") at least once a day this week. See what parts of the chapter speak most strongly to you, and look for opportunities to put the chapter's words into practice with yourself, your neighbors, and God.

Closing Prayer

Living God, help us to walk in the way of love that Jesus modeled for us. As we seek to follow you, help us to be discerning about where our loyalties lie, and show us anything in our hearts and minds that stands in our way of being on mission with you. In Jesus' name. Amen.

Session 3

Toward a Loving God of Liberation

PLANNING THE SESSION

Session Goals

Through this session's discussion and activities, participants will be encouraged to

- discover what it means to embark on the second migration—the theological migration;
- consider how our view of God needs to change and evolve; and
- look to Jesus as the ultimate example of who God is and how we should live.

Preparation

- Read and reflect on "Part II: The Theological Migration: From a Violent God of Domination to a Nonviolent God of Liberation," in *The Great Spiritual Migration: How the World's Largest Religion Is Seeking a Better Way to Be Christian* by Brian McLaren.
- Read through this session outline in its entirety to familiarize yourself with the material being covered. Be aware that there is a lot of material that can be covered within this session, so try to balance your discussion and

group activity times. Choose the session elements you will use during the group session, including the specific discussion questions you plan to cover. Be prepared, however, to adjust the session as group members interact and as questions arise. Prepare carefully, but allow space for the Holy Spirit to move in and through the group members and through you as facilitator.

- Read and reflect on the following Scriptures:
    Genesis 1:28
    Philippians 2:6-11
    John 8:1-11
    Matthew 5:17
    2 Peter 1:5-7
    Hebrews 1:1-3
    Colossians 1:15, 19-20
    1 Corinthians 13
- Have a markerboard or large sheet of paper available for recording group members' ideas.
- Have a Bible, paper for taking notes, and a pen or pencil available for every participant.

OPENING ACTIVITY AND PRAYER (5–10 MINUTES)

For discussion:

- Last week's call to action was to focus on love by reading 1 Corinthians 13 repeatedly and looking for opportunities to put the Scripture into practice (with yourself, your neighbors, and God). Would anyone like to share any experiences or thoughts you had while putting these principles into practice?

Read aloud or summarize:

In the last session, we discussed McLaren's call for Christianity to migrate spiritually. In this session, we are going to discuss the need for Christianity to begin a theological migration.

Opening Prayer

Eternal God, as we gather together today, help us to see your glory as we've never seen it before. Help us to have courage to look to our past, present, and future to have a greater understanding of what it means to follow you and to be faithful to your message. We know that you are here with us today, and we thank you for your attentiveness to us. In Jesus' name. Amen.

DVD Segment (15 minutes)

Study and Discussion (35–40 minutes)

The "Genocide Card"

(Note to the Leader: This session deals with some hard truths about the history of Christianity and its traditional oppression of minorities. As you discuss, be sensitive to those in your group who may have experienced this kind of oppression firsthand. Proceed gently and be aware, taking special care to guide the conversation with these members in mind.)

Read aloud or summarize:

It's not news to us that we live in a violent world. With the ever-increasing news coverage and quick reporting from all corners of the world, we are constantly aware of the countless tragedies and conflicts that people are facing on a daily basis. It is hard to take in and to process.

In chapter 4 of *The Great Spiritual Migration,* McLaren shines a light on Christianity's violent history. As early Christianity spread throughout the world, it unfortunately became infiltrated by and wrapped up in political power plays. Leaders claimed the "dominion mandate" found in Genesis 1:28 and distorted it for their own purposes. Countless rulers and politicians and even clergy took their idea of a vengeful, warring God, and turned the faith into a weapon meant to subdue and dominate.

For discussion:

McLaren writes:

> If Christian faith is to experience the great spiritual migration it needs, our cover-ups and denial must be replaced with humble awareness and a deep change of heart, because the less aware Christians are of how dangerous Christianity has been, the more dangerous Christianity will be. It's been said that the truth will set you free, but first it will probably make you mad. That's the case for this chapter.

- As you read this chapter, what made you mad or sad? Is there one event mentioned that particularly broke your heart?
- Have you ever considered Christianity's violent history? How does it make you feel to learn more about this? How does it give you a different perspective on how Christians are sometimes viewed by other cultures or religions?

Read aloud Genesis 1:28:

> *God blessed them and said to them, "Be fertile and multiply; fill the earth and master it. Take charge of the fish of the sea, the birds in the sky, and everything crawling on the ground."*
>
> *Genesis 1:28*

Read aloud or summarize:

McLaren points out that many have taken this verse and twisted its original intention into what became known as Pope Nicholas V's Doctrine of Discovery, written in 1452, which said that Christians were allowed—the implication being *ordained*—to take control of anything and anyone they "discovered" in their explorations. This justification opened the door to slavery, abuse, and domination of native peoples by establishing Christians and Christianity as supreme over others. As a result, egregious acts were perpetrated on indigenous peoples, with few people even speaking out against these horrible acts. McLaren calls this declaration the "genocide card."

For discussion:

- Do you agree with McLaren's conclusions that, for many, Christianity has allowed people to carry the "genocide card" in their back pockets? How do you react to that statement?
- For most of us, at first, this idea probably seems too harsh—after all, we are far removed from those violent histories and the people who carried them out. But as you thought and read more about this idea—that many who claim Christianity have bought into the idea of their supremacy and domination, perhaps in much more subtle, but still dangerous, ways—can you see how McLaren's point is valid?
- Have you seen or experienced any subtle, or not so subtle, displays of "Christian" supremacy? If so, how, and what was your reaction or observation?
- What do you think the people who wrote and followed the Doctrine of Discovery thought about God? About Genesis 1:28?
- Today we Christians tend to think of other religions as much more violent than Christianity. How do McLaren's

reflections change your view of that notion and of people who practice other religions?

The Doctrine of White Christian Privilege

Read aloud or summarize:

In current-day America and in many other places around the world, McLaren points out, many of us still adhere to the "Doctrine of White Christian Privilege." A history of slavery and systemic discrimination affects our country still today, and the doctrine is one that many Christians follow without truly thinking about how we buy into the mindset. Read the quote from Professor Yolanda Pierce of the Princeton Theological Seminary in chapter 4 of *The Great Spiritual Migration*. She asks, "Can this nation afford to keep ignoring the truth that black people in American live under a threat of racial violence, never quite feeling that we are fully equal citizens in the nation that our enslaved ancestors built?"

McLaren points out that it is important that we in the church begin to acknowledge that we don't draw the same extreme conclusions that our ancestors did (for example, slavery and civil discrimination), but that we must realize our religion still too often interprets the Bible as they did. He writes, "If we face our past, we will see how many power centers within the Christian community still carry white Christian supremacy and white Christian privilege cards in their back pocket, often without even knowing they do so, and as a result can be found consistently allying themselves with oppressors rather than the oppressed."

For discussion:

- What do you think about what Yolanda Pierce had to say about theological white supremacy still reigning in our churches today?

- Does your faith community discuss how your theology responds to race relations? If not, why do you think that is?
- McLaren recounts the story of his grandfather, whom he loved and considered a wonderful man of faith, though his grandfather held on to racism throughout his life, which deeply grieves McLaren. Have you had similar experiences with family members or friends? How have you responded?
- In chapter 4, McLaren quotes a Native American scholar who asserted that, based on the Christianity her people have known, she does not believe the religion is even salvageable. Why do you think she says this? What is your reaction to her statement? (If you immediately feel defensive about that observation, try to put yourself in the shoes of someone who has faced persecution or dismissal in the name of "Christian principles." In that light, how do you view that statement? Does it give you a different perspective or insight?)

God 5.0

Read aloud or summarize:

As we mature from infant to child to adolescent to adult, our conceptions of God grow and develop over time and with maturity. McLaren notes these stages of development in chapter 5, leading up to what he says we desperately need—a next-level view of God, which he calls "God 5.0."

On the way to this new vision of God 5.0, we go through several stages:

1. God 1.0 – the God you can trust, the way an infant trusts a parent or caregiver
2. God 2.0 – the God who encourages you to be polite and generous and play well with others

3. God 3.0 – the God who rewards the rule-keepers and punishes the rule-breakers
4. God 4.0 – the God of affection and family, of the *exclusive we*, the one who takes care of all of us—but not those who have different beliefs

For discussion:

- Where do you think you (or your faith community) fall within these developmental stages and why?

Read aloud or summarize:

Why do we need to adopt a new, or updated, version of God? Perhaps a better question is, why would we *not* seek to deepen our knowledge of God?

Just as in the last session we discussed the scientific method of changing facts in light of new information, the same often needs to happen in our spiritual growth. Because we can look back at how our ancestors used Scripture as justification for domination and subjugation, we can reject their interpretation of God and Scripture, and replace that interpretation with a wiser form. McLaren writes, "We are coming to see in the life and teaching of Christ, and especially in the cross and resurrection of Christ, *a radical rejection of dominating supremacy in all its forms.*" We need a new way. And in order to do that, we first need to examine the true picture of supremacy—Jesus.

Read aloud Philippians 2:6-11:

> *Though he was in the form of God,*
> *he did not consider being equal with God*
> *something to exploit.*
> *But he emptied himself*
> *by taking the form of a slave*
> *and by becoming like human beings.*

> *When he found himself in the form of a human,*
> *he humbled himself by becoming obedient to*
> *the point of death,*
> *even death on a cross.*
> *Therefore, God highly honored him*
> *and gave him a name above all names,*
> *so that at the name of Jesus everyone*
> *in heaven, on earth, and under the earth*
> *might bow*
> *and every tongue confess that*
> *Jesus Christ is Lord, to the glory of God*
> *the Father.*
>
> *Philippians 2:6-11*

For discussion:

- When we look back into our past and consider the actions of many powerful people, we see them clinging to whatever tactics would give them the power. Jesus, writes McLaren, "ultimately overturned all conventional understandings of supremacy, lordship, sovereignty, and power by purging them of violence—to the point where he himself chose to be killed rather than kill. In this way, according to Philippians 2, Jesus manifested the true nature or image of God." As you read Philippians 2:6-11, what words describing Jesus stand out to you? Do you find yourself surprised by any of them?
- Throughout his ministry, Jesus empowered others, rejected violence and domination, overturned conventional ideas of supremacy and power, and was anything but a conquering king. Read aloud John 8:1-11. What qualities of leadership do we see Jesus displaying here?

*And Jesus went to the Mount of Olives. Early in the
morning he returned to the temple. All the people
gathered around him, and he sat down and taught
them. The legal experts and Pharisees brought a woman
caught in adultery. Placing her in the center of the group,
they said to Jesus, "Teacher, this woman was caught
in the act of committing adultery. In the Law, Moses
commanded us to stone women like this. What do you
say?" They said this to test him, because they wanted a
reason to bring an accusation against him. Jesus bent
down and wrote on the ground with his finger.*

*They continued to question him, so he stood up and
replied, "Whoever hasn't sinned should throw the
first stone." Bending down again, he wrote on the
ground. Those who heard him went away, one by one,
beginning with the elders. Finally, only Jesus and the
woman were left in the middle of the crowd.*

*Jesus stood up and said to her, "Woman, where are
they? Is there no one to condemn you?"*

She said, "No one, sir."

*Jesus said, "Neither do I condemn you. Go, and from
now on, don't sin anymore."*

John 8:1-11

Read aloud or summarize:

Throughout his ministry, Jesus can be seen empowering others,
rejecting others' ideas about the kind of leader he should be, and
putting himself on the line in defense of others time and time
again. And so, if we are to follow Jesus, whom God sent to lead
us, then it reasons that we must look beyond the image of the God

who is dominating and angry and change that image, because Jesus brought a radical new vision of God to the earth.

This new understanding is what McLaren calls God 5.0. The God of the *inclusive we*—the God not just for *some* of us, but for *all of us*. In order for us to move forward with the understanding that we are all one family and need to take care of each other and the earth as well, we have to embrace God 5.0. This is the theological migration we need.

McLaren is quick to point out, however, that migrating to and embracing God 5.0 doesn't mean that we abandon what is in the Bible. This isn't a wholesale rejection and replacement, but an integral, step-by-step change. McLaren writes:

> We see this pattern in the Scriptures. When Moses is given the Ten Commandments, he doesn't say that Abraham's religion was wrong because he didn't have them. And when Solomon builds an elaborate temple of stone, he doesn't say Moses's religion was wrong because he had only a tent of cloth. And when the prophets Amos, Isaiah, and Micah come along, they don't advocate rejecting their religion and culture, even though they are highly critical of its spiritual hypocrisy and social injustice. They want their religion to expand, to evolve, to learn and grow. The same is true with Jesus. He came, he said, not to abolish or replace, but to fulfill what came before him.

For discussion:

- What is your reaction to McLaren's view that we need a new interpretation of God? Is this idea of theological migration new to you?

- Have you ever considered that it is okay for your religion to evolve or expand? Has anyone in your faith community ever challenged you in that regard? How does that idea make you feel? Excited? defensive? skeptical? engaged?

- Read Matthew 5:17. What new vision of God did Jesus give us?

   "Do not think that I have come to abolish the law or the prophets; I have come not to abolish but to fulfill."
   Matthew 5:17 (NRSV)

- Read 2 Peter 1:5-7. How does this Scripture speak to theological evolution?

   This is why you must make every effort to add moral excellence to your faith; and to moral excellence, knowledge; and to knowledge, self-control; and to self-control, endurance; and to endurance, godliness; and to godliness, affection for others; and to affection for others, love.
   2 Peter 1:5-7

Read aloud Hebrews 1:1-3 and Colossians 1:15, 19-20:

   Long ago God spoke to our ancestors in many and various ways by the prophets, but in these last days he has spoken to us by a Son, whom he appointed heir of all things, through whom he also created the worlds. He is the reflection of God's glory and the exact imprint of God's very being.
   Hebrews 1:1-3 (NRSV)

> *[Christ] is the image of the invisible God, the*
> *firstborn of all creation; . . . For in him all the fullness*
> *of God was pleased to dwell, and through him God*
> *was pleased to reconcile to himself all things, whether*
> *on earth or in heaven, by making peace through the*
> *blood of his cross.*
>
> *Colossians 1:15, 19-20 (NRSV)*

For discussion:

- What do these verses have to say about the importance of Jesus?
- Hebrews 1:1-2 says, "Long ago God spoke to our ancestors in many and various ways by the prophets, but in these last days he has spoken to us by a Son" (NRSV). Jesus is the "last word," so to speak. What impression, then, do you believe God wants to give us about what kind of leader God is?

CLOSING ACTIVITY AND PRAYER (5 MINUTES)

Leader, as you close each week's session, plan to take a few minutes for participants to quietly reflect on what you have discussed during this session. A reflection question or questions will be provided each week, along with a closing Call to Action, which participants will be invited to receive and engage in between meetings.

Read aloud or summarize:

- In what ways do you think your view of God and/or the Bible needs to change?

Call to Action

In this part of the book, we are being challenged to see how our view of God is slowly maturing. Referring back to the stages of development of our knowledge of God (God 1.0, 2.0, and so on, as detailed in chapter 5 of *The Great Spiritual Migration*), reflect on your own journey of how your view of God has matured. Think through each stage and what experiences brought you to each new stage of awareness. Where are you today?

Closing Prayer

God, help us to see you most clearly through your Son, Jesus. Help us to embrace and be transformed into his image, reflecting his glory to others so they will see how good and merciful and true and generous you are. Allow us to be changed, Living God, and let that change happen without fear, for you ask us to walk confidently in your presence. In Jesus' name. Amen.

Session 4

For the Common Good

PLANNING THE SESSION

Session Goals

Through this session's discussion and activities, participants will be encouraged to

- reflect on the way that Jesus began a lasting social movement;
- consider what it means to respond to Jesus' call to "Follow me";
- explore how different gifts and strengths can contribute to the great spiritual migration; and
- run the race that God has laid out for them and to continue on their transformational path.

Preparation

- Read and reflect on "Part III: The Missional Migration: From Organized Religion to Organizing Religion," in *The Great Spiritual Migration: How the World's Largest Religion Is Seeking a Better Way to Be Christian* by Brian McLaren.
- Read through this session outline in its entirety to familiarize yourself with the material being covered. Be aware that there is a lot of material that can be covered within this session, so try to balance your discussion and

group activity times. Choose the session elements you will use during the group session, including the specific discussion questions you plan to cover. Be prepared, however, to adjust the session as group members interact and as questions arise. Prepare carefully, but allow space for the Holy Spirit to move in and through the group members and through you as facilitator.

- Read and reflect on the following Scriptures:
    Matthew 9:9-13
    Mark 3:1-6
    Luke 4:14-30
    John 5:1-18
    Matthew 16:24-25
    Matthew 7:3-5
    1 Peter 2:5
    1 Corinthians 12:12-14
    Romans 12:5-8
    Galatians 4:19
    Hebrews 12:1-2
    Matthew 6:10
- Have a markerboard or large sheet of paper available for recording group members' ideas.
- Have a Bible, paper for taking notes, and a pen or pencil available for every participant.

OPENING ACTIVITY AND PRAYER
(5–10 MINUTES)

For discussion:

- Last week's call to action was to reflect on your own journey of how your view of God has matured over time. Would anyone like to share about any realizations or

52

insights you gained while thinking through your own journey?

Read aloud or summarize:

In the last session, we discussed McLaren's call for Christianity to migrate theologically. In this session, we are going to discuss what it means for Christianity to begin a missional migration, moving from a religion organized for self-preservation to a religion organized for the common good of all.

Opening Prayer

Lord, as we seek a new way to see you and know you, help us to discover more about what it means to live out our faith in a way that is honoring to you. Help us to consider this new way of being as a way to serve and love you and bring your healing to this world. In Jesus' name. Amen.

DVD Segment (15 minutes)

Study and Discussion (35–40 minutes)

Migration as Salvation

Read aloud or summarize:

Along with a migration in our spiritual and theological lives comes the call for a new way of life. Because Christianity is no longer a simple system of beliefs that we live by, the way we express our faith through our actions and our churches needs to migrate as well.

In chapter 7 of *The Great Spiritual Migration*, McLaren spends some time talking about social movement theory. People group into communities, and as communities grow, institutions are organized to help care for the needs of the people. Ideally these institutions function very well for the members of the community, but sometimes these institutions fail or become corrupted. When that happens, members of the community band together to form movements to reform the institutions.

For discussion:

- What are some movements that have happened in the past that you can name? (Examples include the abolitionist movement, the women's suffrage movement, the civil rights movement, and so on.)
- Have you ever been a part of a movement (either on a large or small scale)? What prompted you to get involved in the movement, and what was your experience working within it? Did your efforts result in the change you hoped for?
- Are there any religious movements that you have been involved with or are aware of? What were or are the goals of those movements?

Read aloud or summarize:

We don't tend to think about it this way, but what Jesus did in his ministry was begin a social movement. He came to earth to minister and teach and sacrifice to show that change was coming.

Activity:

Read the following four Scripture passages with the group, one from each Gospel of the New Testament: Matthew 9:9-13, Mark 3:1-6, Luke 4:14-30, and John 5:1-18. Read the passages aloud and answer the following questions. (If your group is large, you might want to break into smaller groups and assign each group one passage.)

For each passage, ask:

- In this passage, what social/cultural norm or institution did Jesus challenge?
- What part did his disciples (or the community of people who followed him) play in this scene?
- How did institutional leaders react to Jesus' actions? What challenge did Jesus issue to them?

Follow Me

Read aloud Matthew 16:24-25:

> *Then Jesus said to his disciples, "All who want to come after me must say no to themselves, take up their cross, and follow me. All who want to save their lives will lose them. But all who lose their lives because of me will find them."*
>
> Matthew 16:24-25

Read aloud or summarize:

Jesus' message was certainly countercultural to the institutional, organized religion of his day. It was a dangerous social movement, to be sure, and yet many followed him willingly. In this passage from the Gospel of Matthew, Jesus offers strong words to the disciples who are following him, which must have left them wondering what in the world he was talking about. Did he mean actual, physical death? Maybe, since it was a dangerous time to be challenging the reigning authority of the day. But his words also held a great promise: "All who lose their lives because of me will find them" (Matthew 16:25). Jesus was saying that change was coming, and there was a life better than they could imagine at the end of this life.

For discussion:

- How would you describe Jesus' call to you as his disciple? Is there anything you have felt you needed to let go of in your pursuit of Jesus?

Read aloud or summarize:

To be a disciple of Jesus is to be a part of a vast community that is committed to living lives bigger than themselves. Is it time for the church's life to be lost, in order to be found? McLaren asks, "Could our desire to save our precious religious institutions and traditions actually hasten their demise? Could it be that the spirit of God is calling the church to stop trying to save itself, and instead to join God in saving the world? Could pouring out itself for the good of the world be the only way for the church to save its own soul?"

In the DVD segment, McLaren tells the story of the man next to him on a plane who said that organized religion wasn't "his cup of tea" and who went on to point out all the ways in which organized religion has failed to truly care for others and for our earth. This man's perspective can tell us a lot about how many today view the church, and we should not run from this insight. McLaren writes, "That's why we so desperately need this third migration: from *a religion organized for self-preservation and privilege to a religion organizing for the common good of all.*"

For discussion:

- Do you see the need for Christianity to essentially reorganize, to move toward organizing for the common good? In what areas do you think this migration is most needed?
- How do you think these changes would affect our communities, our country, and our world?

Read aloud or summarize:

Perhaps you've seen a bumper sticker or poster that says, "Be the change you want to see in the world." It's a powerful quote, often misattributed to Mahatma Gandhi, but what Gandhi said was even more enlightening: "If we could change ourselves, the tendencies in the world would also change. As a man changes his own nature, so does the attitude of the world change towards him. . . . We need not wait to see what others do."*

This is certainly true for us as followers of Christ.

Read Matthew 7:3-5 and 1 Peter 2:5:

> *Why do you see the splinter that's in your brother's or sister's eye, but don't notice the log in your own eye? How can you say to your brother or sister, 'Let me take the splinter out of your eye,' when there's a log in your eye? You deceive yourself! First take the log out of your eye, and then you'll see clearly to take the splinter out of your brother's or sister's eye.*
>
> *Matthew 7:3-5*

> *You yourselves are being built like living stones into a spiritual temple. You are being made into a holy priesthood to offer up spiritual sacrifices that are acceptable to God through Jesus Christ.*
>
> *1 Peter 2:5*

For discussion:

- What would happen to our world (and our religion) if we addressed the same greed, fear, anger, and apathy in our hearts that is in our world? What changes would and could happen?

---

* Brian Morton, "Falser Words Were Never Spoken," *The New York Times*, August 29, 2011, http://www.nytimes.com/2011/08/30/opinion/falser-words-were-never-spoken.html.

- We are the "living stones" of 1 Peter, and are being called to look within to examine our own role as a piece of our religion's spiritual temple. When Jesus claimed in John 2 that he would destroy the Temple, he wasn't making a statement against the Jewish faith but claiming God's desire to dwell within the human heart instead. How does the knowledge that you are a "living stone," with the important responsibility of supporting God's work in the world, change your perspective on being a disciple?
- In terms of environmental responsibility, what role do you think the church should play? How should we as disciples influence that conversation?

Where Do We Go From Here?

Read aloud or summarize:

McLaren points out that the pattern of organizing and reorganizing has occurred throughout Christian history (for example, David replaced Saul, Luther began the Protestant Reformation, and the Jesus Movement of the 60s and 70s became widespread). So where do we go from here? McLaren proposes a migration "from a religion organized for self-preservation and privilege to a religion organizing for the common good of all."

Toward this migration, McLaren presents the following charges:

1. Christian communities that are engaging this migration should speak up, and other Christians should start new communities where there are none.
2. Christian leaders and parents should start with children and young people so that they are familiar with the ideas of the movement from the beginning.
3. Christian communities should get different leaders and train them differently (and without debt where possible).

For discussion:

- What are your thoughts or reactions to these charges?
- How are you (and/or your community) already engaging in some of these charges? In what areas do you need to dig deeper? Which do you see as most challenging?

Read aloud or summarize:

McLaren declares that Christianity is salvageable, but it will certainly take our careful thought and effort to save it. If we can embrace these migrations and become relevant and transformational in the world, McLaren sees our impact spreading in four ways:

1. intrapersonal (within each person),
2. interpersonal (between people),
3. structural/institutional (creating structures that protect and nourish people), and
4. cultural (implementing real change on a widespread level).

For discussion:

- How was Jesus' ministry impactful in the four ways listed above?
- In *The Great Spiritual Migration,* McLaren quotes Pope Francis, who referred to those committed to caring for all people left behind as "social poets," and expressed his solidarity with them. What are some ways that followers of Jesus can better become "social poets" and lead this charge?

Many Gifts, One Body

Read aloud or summarize:

As McLaren points out, Jesus' social movement was full of diversity. Women were highly active, and his close disciples varied greatly in gifts and temperament—John was a poet, Simon a Zealot, Peter an organizer. This fact celebrates the diversity that we should celebrate in Christianity as well.

Read aloud 1 Corinthians 12:12-14 and Romans 12:5-8:

> *Christ is just like the human body—a body is a unit and has many parts; and all the parts of the body are one body, even though there are many. We were all baptized by one Spirit into one body, whether Jew or Greek, or slave or free, and we all were given one Spirit to drink. Certainly the body isn't one part but many.*
>
> *1 Corinthians 12:12-14*

> *In the same way, though there are many of us, we are one body in Christ, and individually we belong to each other. We have different gifts that are consistent with God's grace that has been given to us. If your gift is prophecy, you should prophesy in proportion to your faith. If your gift is service, devote yourself to serving. If your gift is teaching, devote yourself to teaching. If your gift is encouragement, devote yourself to encouraging. The one giving should do it with no strings attached. The leader should lead with passion. The one showing mercy should be cheerful.*
>
> *Romans 12:5-8*

Read aloud or summarize:

Both of these passages depict Christ as a living body, made up of many parts. It takes all of us—with our imperfections and doubts and fears and strengths—to make up the movement of the church and to embark on this migration. Everyone is essential.

For discussion:

- How does your faith community celebrate and utilize the different strengths of its members? Are there ways that it could improve?
- How can this idea of celebrating others' differing gifts and utilizing their strengths be extended beyond your community into other denominations?
- In *The Great Spiritual Migration,* McLaren asks, what if this was extended even further, to include different religions? He writes, "I believe the Holy Spirit has brought us to this point where, in order to grapple with the threat of ecological, economic, societal, and spiritual self-destruction, we must for the first time in history receive the differing gifts each tradition offers." He says that we should do this, not to try and convert or be converted, but to be committed to changes of heart in *every* person toward the common good. For such a movement to succeed, multifaith collaboration is essential. What do you think about this idea? Have you ever seen this type of collaboration? If so, what was the result?

Running the Race

Read aloud or summarize:

Christianity is certainly salvageable, but it will take all of us, working together, to save it, says McLaren. It won't be an easy road, and there will certainly be tough opposition along the way.

In Galatians 4:19, Paul, coaching the young Galatian church, writes, "I'm going through labor pains again until Christ is formed in you." McLaren writes, "For a new and better world to be born, for our faith to experience a deep change of heart, for the great spiritual migration we need to become a reality, someone must be willing to suffer birth pains, and those pains will often come in the form of criticism and personal attack." Those are the moments that we should hold tightly to God on the path God has asked us to walk.

Read aloud Hebrews 12:1-2 and Matthew 6:10.

> *So then let's also run the race that is laid out in front of us, since we have such a great cloud of witnesses surrounding us. Let's throw off any extra baggage, get rid of the sin that trips us up, and fix our eyes on Jesus, faith's pioneer and perfecter. He endured the cross, ignoring the shame, for the sake of the joy that was laid out in front of him, and sat down at the right side of God's throne.*
>
>

Hebrews 12:1-2

> *Your kingdom come.*
> *Your will be done,*
> > *on earth as it is in heaven.*
>
>

Matthew 6:10 (NRSV)

For discussion:

- What race do you see your faith community called to run? In order to run well and faithfully, what "extra baggage" do you need to get rid of? From what sin that trips you up do you need to repent?
- McLaren believes the purpose of the church is to join God in the healing of the world, and that healing needs to begin within us. How are you feeling called into this purpose?
- McLaren ends the book with the encouragement that the importance of embarking on this migration shouldn't cause us to feel the weight of the world on our shoulders, but to realize that "we are but children at play with God,

living in a world where everything is holy. That is liberation spirituality." Why do you think he chooses to end the book on this note? How does this comment encourage or challenge you in your own spiritual migration?

CLOSING ACTIVITY AND PRAYER (5 MINUTES)

Leader, as you close this week's session, plan to take a few minutes for participants to quietly reflect on what you have discussed during this session. A reflection question is provided, along with a closing Call to Action, which participants will be invited to receive and engage in as your study closes.

Read aloud or summarize:

- How are you feeling at the end of this book and this study? In what areas is God stirring your heart into action?

(*Note to Leader*: If you wish, take a few minutes for participants to quietly reflect on this question and journal their thoughts.)

Call to Action

As this study ends, keep the momentum and your discussion going. Find a buddy who is also committed to this migration and make an action plan about next steps moving forward. Perhaps you want to dive into a deeper study in one area? Start a discussion group? Organize an event that helps you get to know the people in your community and their needs better? Make one small step that can help you move forward in your journey.

Closing Prayer

Living God, break our hearts open for the things that matter to you. Direct our steps and help us to draw on your strength as we move forward in faith. Help us to serve in sync with the movement of your Spirit. In Jesus' name. Amen.